the break of daun...

my transformation

Daun Long Pittman

the break of daun...

Printed in the USA

ISBN – 9798594653382

This book recounts the events in the life of Daun Long Pittman according to the author's recollection and perspective. While all stories are true, some names and details have been excluded to protect the privacy of those involved.

Editor - My Aunt, Shirley Washington, my dad's precious sister

Book Cover Photography – daughter PresLee Pittman

Butterfly Illustration - daughter HeartLee Pittman

Dedication

I feel incredibly honored to have the privilege of dedicating this book to the one and only, *Mamie Lee Glover Cook*, my 99-year-old grandmother, whom I call, *Big Mother*. Her name really does not accurately describe her, since she is a tiny little lady, probably five-foot or less, but she most certainly has a *big* heart! On occasion when I can spend time with her, she always reminds me that I am her only granddaughter, and that she loves me very, very much. The Apostle Paul quotes the commandment in his letter to the church in Epistle to the Ephesians/Ephesus and says, "Children, if you want to be wise, listen to your parents and do what they tell you, and the Lord will help you." For the commandment, "Honor your father and your mother," was the first of the Ten Commandments with a promise attached: "You will prosper and live a long, full life if you honor your parents." This verse is found in Ephesians 6:1-3. So, evidently my grandmother must have done something right to have lived such a wonderful, prosperous, and healthy life. She is someone greatly to be admired. As a child I will never forget following her every footstep and listening to all the many stories she would tell. Back in the day she worked full time and I recall running out to meet her on the dirt road as she pulled up in the late afternoons. She would cook a huge Sunday meal and put it all on the table for everyone to enjoy and then put a tablecloth over the food until dinner that night. She would lovingly sing me a lullaby before going to sleep at night.

Go to sleep little baby,

before the Boogie Man gets you.

When you wake, I'll give you some cake.

And all the pretty little horse, and all the pretty

little horses.

I love you so very, very much Big Mother. Both you and Bobby are a tremendous blessing to me and my daughters. Thank you for all your many prayers and unconditional love that you pour out on others. May God bless you and give you many more years here on earth.

Forward

Anji Johnson

Friends 4 Life

I have known Daun for over 36 years. We have been there for each other through all our ups and downs in life. She always had a bubbly personality filled with confidence and encouragement. Her walk in Christ always showed in everything she did in life. When I first met Daun, she took me under her wings. You see, I was a very shy person with no confidence and low self-esteem, and somehow, she helped give me the courage to stand in front of a crowd of my peers and sing my heart out. As the years have passed, Daun has encouraged many shy people, with low self-esteem, and helped build their confidence in themselves. She has left a trail of God's love and compassion with everyone she meets.

But then one day, it all changed. Daun's smile and laughter went away. I saw, but only a shell of an old friend. This book takes you on her journey, a rollercoaster ride of emotions as she opens up her heart and pours out her personal pain of rejection and heartache. Through this, Daun's faith in God was always in the middle of it all. When she wanted to give up, her faith promised a better day. She shares how, at times, she felt abandoned by God, not only was she and her daughters forced to leave their home, but she had to find another job and create a new beginning all while mourning the loss of her father. Through scripture and the power of prayer, Daun has overcome many obstacles. I can see and hear my old friend again and God is rewriting a beautiful new life, filled with smiles and laughter.

When I first met my co-worker and friend Daun, about one year ago, she was brokenhearted. I'm reminded of the scripture, Psalm 34:18, which says, "The Lord is close to the brokenhearted and saves those who are crushed in spirit." And though she was broken, she drew her strength by drawing close to the Lord and what an amazing transformation! She is no longer the person that I first met. As she sowed tears in seeking Him, the Lord watered and allowed her to grow in strength. She has an amazing light within her that reflects who she is in Christ – she is radiant and has blossomed. She is joyful and a beautiful person inside and out and I am blessed to be called her sister in Christ!

Julia Manuel

Co-Worker and Wonderful Friend

Daun and I connected over our love for God and family. I absolutely love her positive outlook on life. I remember thinking this is the sweetest, praying lady I know. She stayed with her prayer book in her hands. I could tell that she was broken...I recognized that look personally. She later shared her marital story of how she was betrayed and abandoned. I saw and felt her pain as she began to weep. She expressed how she felt that she was a failure... that she had failed in her marriage, her kids, her career, and herself.

There are five stages to grief... denial, anger, bargaining, depression, and anger. As she navigated her way through each stage, she was reminded of Psalm 30:5, that "Weeping may endure for a night, but joy comes in the morning." The pain that she endured during that dark season catapulted her into her purpose as a writer, motivator, and encourager. I literally watched her bloom. She regained her strength. She began to pray bold prayers and expected great and mighty things.

This book highlights Daun's journey from the life she once had, to a life she never knew she needed. She tells personal accounts of what it felt like to have it all and lose it, and declares, if you cry out to God, He will hear you and answer your prayers! In the end, she finds herself, her voice, her passions,

Kitoria Gibbs
Co-Worker Bestie
& Lifesaver

and a renewed love and total dependency for God. Her story is a true example of how God will turn your ashes into beauty.

Growing up with Daun, as my big sister, was always exciting. From kidnapping her Barbies with my Creature from the Black Lagoon Action Figure, to being a Cast Member in her, *what seemed to be daily*, Impromptu, "*Broadwayesque*" Performances. I understood as a kid, how lucky I was to have her as a sister and playmate. Now, as an adult, I understand she was *much more than that.* I have never met another person as selfless, compassionate and loving, as Daun. Her life has been a shining testimony pointing me straight to Jesus, then... as her baby brother, and now... as a husband and father of three grown kids.

There is no doubt that God blessed me in an exceedingly abundant way making Daun my big sister!!! This book will be as honest, kind, and loving as she is, and will point you directly to Jesus.

When I married David, I had no idea that I was going to inherit a genuinely beautiful and Godly sister-in-law. Daun has truly been a wonderful Aunt to my children, the most thoughtful and selfless sister and friend to me and a rock for my husbands' entire family. She has a heart of gold and has never hesitated to help me through tough times of my own. Over the years, I've watched Daun become a mother, a schoolteacher, a caretaker, a friend, an encourager, a singer...but the most important characteristic of Daun has always remained the same, she is a child of God and that shines through in everything that she does. Her books will offer a small glimpse into her life and what it means to let Christ be at the center of everything and your prayer life. I hope that everyone enjoys Daun's daily sprinkles of inspiration as well as her touching and heart-warming stories of her life experiences as much as I do.

Kristin and David

Sis-N-Luv and Little Brother

Daun is a wonderful sister for who I am so thankful. She is a dedicated faithful Christian woman who has always put family, friends, and people ahead of her own needs. My sister is the greatest example of Godliness and love that I know. You are my Hero! Love Danny

Daun is one of the strongest examples of being a true Christian that I know. She earnestly tries to follow God's teaching and help others along the way. A true Christian spirit and I'm fortunate to have her as a sister-n-law.

Danny and Sharon

Big Brother and Sister-N-Law

I am not sure that I deserve such kindhearted words from all these special people in my life.

But...

I am sure that this makes me more determined than ever to be an Ambassador for Christ, keeping Him in the center of my life, and striving to be more and more like Him every day.

"But let me tell you something wonderful, a mystery I'll probably never fully understand. We're not all going to die – but we are all going to be changed."

1 Corinthians 15:51

Introduction 

There is something quite whimsical about a butterfly dancing in the sky. It is extremely captivating to observe the beauty of God's handiwork. I love the way The Message Bible interprets what David said in Psalm 19:1,2 "God's glory is on tour in the skies, God-craft on exhibit across the horizon. Madame Day holds classes every morning, Professor Night lectures each evening." In the midst of all Gods glorious creation, He places a beautiful symbol to soar through the Heavens representing endurance, change, hope, resurrection and life. The transformation of a butterfly is simply fascinating – how it starts out as a tiny plant bound creature, eating its way through a relatively monotonous existence. When suddenly, something deep inside this little critter receives a message that it is time to change. The caterpillar begins to wrap itself in a silk blanket as if to say, "goodnight, sweet dreams".

Then the mysterious transformation begins to take place. You may think that the little worm with legs is simply hibernating in a cocoon, but what is happening is even more miraculous than that. Once encased in a chrysalis the caterpillar releases enzymes that turn its body into liquid. From this watery substance the entire creature is rebuilt. The muscles, the nervous system, the heart, everything is completely recreated. Suddenly, its life is forever changed. The lowly caterpillar transforms into a brilliant butterfly.

And if such transformation can happen with God's creatures, why not with people. Can we undergo an inner metamorphosis just as wonderous and amazing as the outward transformations we see in nature? The answer is yes! 2 Corinthians 5:17 says, "Therefore if any man be in Christ, he is a new creature: old things are passed away; behold, all things are become new." Just as the caterpillar was not meant to remain a caterpillar, we were not meant to remain stagnant. And as the butterfly emerges as a fragile, vulnerable creature, it possesses an unimaginable freedom – the freedom to fly. Like the butterfly, God wants to grow us, transform us, and strengthen our wings so that we can also take flight.

Oh yes, you shaped me first inside, then out;

You formed me in my mother's womb.

I thank You, Father God – You're breathtaking!

Body and soul, I am marvelously made!

I worship in adoration- what a creation!

You know me inside and out,

you know every bone in my body;

You know exactly how I was made, bit by bit,

how I was sculpted from nothing into something.

Like an open book, you watched me grow from conception.

to birth; all the stages of my life were spread out before

you, the days of my life all prepared

before I'd even lived one day.

Psalm 139: 15, 16

Compelled by an unknown force I followed my instinct and retreated into the darkness. I was searching for my personal refuge and felt safe in familiar surroundings. Without an ounce of strength left in my limbs, I could no longer continue to hold myself up. There was no oxygen left inside these lungs and I gasped for every breath. My bones protruded from my skin and my abdomen begged for nourishment. It was bitterly cold, so I nestled myself in a soft, silk blanket. The stench of death unleashed a shadow around me. As my frail body lay broken in its ugliest, quietest, seemingly weakest and most vulnerable state, deep down in my soul, I sensed it was time to change. There was complete silence in the madness and my body hoped this would be a place of rest. Little did I know, this metamorphosis would forever change my life.

2 Corinthians 3:18 says, "And so we are transfigured much like the Messiah, our lives gradually becoming brighter and more beautiful as God enters our lives and we become like Him." As God began to prepare me for the inexplicable transformation, I closed my eyes, as if to say, "Good night, sweet dreams".

Contents

Chapter 1 

Tribute

In the stillness, my life seemed to flash before my eyes. The part of my brain that stores memories seemed to be the only organ functioning. It was quite phenomenal as if I were reexperiencing my own life events. So many memories and thoughts whirled through my head. Thoughts of my mom, dad, and brothers flooded my mind and I even revisited my childhood. My mom and dad were married on July 4, 1959, on Independence Day, and soon were blessed with a beautiful, blonde haired baby boy they named, Daniel Robert Long Jr. From an early age my parents noticed that he was a perfectionist. He could build model cars and planes and display them all over his room. In fact, his room was that of perfection itself and if anyone messed it up, he would cry and cry and cry. More than anything my mom dreamed of giving him a little sister. Sadly, she had several miscarriages and did not know if her dream would ever be fulfilled. But, five years later by the grace of God, my mom delivered a precious baby girl, who by the way, would be me. The doctors, so they tell me, had never seen a child with such big eyes, and called me 'Bright Eyes' during my short stay in the hospital.

My dad was in the Air Force and traveled the world. We moved every year or two and never stayed in one place very long. My mother was a stay at home mom, and we lived a content and happy life. My brother Danny absolutely loved and protected me. It has been said that if he ever went to the store and got candy, he always would have to get a piece for Daun Lee. That's what he always called me. Who would have thought that seven years later, we would welcome little David into our world, and I would become the middle child? We always called him Da Do (day doo), he was the baby and of course.... the favorite. Lol He was what I call a 'paci' baby. Yes, he loved his pacifier, but then again, who wouldn't enjoy a honey dipped paci 'at your service'. Lol Needless to say, we were a close-knit family. Though we were not by any means a perfect or wealthy family, we were richly loved and perfectly taken care of.

Christianity played an important role in my parents' lives. They both grew up in church, went to the same school, and were elementary school sweethearts. ladadadadadada I remember my grandfather, Daddy Long, being a powerful prayer warrior and would pray for many hours in his bedroom before going to sleep at night. He also left his television on Christian stations where the Word of God was being taught. He spoke God's Word continually to us when we would visit. I believe those prayers and anointed Words planted seeds in my family's lives and God is continuing to water those seeds daily. Isaiah 55:11 explains it better, "So shall my word be that goes out from my mouth; it shall not return to me empty, but it shall accomplish that which I purpose, and shall succeed in the thing for which I sent It". In other words, when we pray and speak God's Words, it is living and powerful. Never does it simply "go out" of our mouth and stop. It is a creative force that sets eternal actions in motion. Though my Grandfather is no longer with us; his prayers are still active and flowing.

When I was little, we went to church on Base, where we lived, and my parents would allow me to partake in communion. This church served real wine during the service and I couldn't wait to tell my friends that I drank wine from a little cup. Lol That is all I remember about church attending, except for going to vacation bible school every summer. I'll never forget one particular summer, my VBS teacher made us hold up our right hand and "Solemnly Swear" to memorize Psalm 23. Seriously? I was only 7 years old, in my eyes this seemed problematic. Who would have thought years later in my mid 20's I would remember the promise that I had made and keep it? Not only did I memorize Psalm 23, I taught hundreds of students over the years to recite it also.

Through the years God would continually tug at my family's heart. God led us to a new town, new faces, and a new church. My whole family got saved, meaning, we asked Christ to come and live inside our hearts. Romans 10:9 says, "That if thou shalt confess with thy mouth the Lord Jesus, and shalt believe in thine heart that God has raised Him from the dead, thou shalt be saved." In order to be saved we must first realize our true state of sinfulness before God and know that He alone can save us, cleanse us, and give us eternal life. FYI, God loved you so much that He made a way for you, through the shed blood of His son so that you might be able to spend eternity with Him. John 3:16 says, "For God so loved the world that He gave His only Begotten Son, that whosoever believeth in Him should not perish, but have Everlasting Life." If you simply need Jesus today, here is a simple prayer to pray...

Dear Lord God, I realize that I am a sinner and have broken your laws. I understand that my sin has separated me from you. I am sorry and I ask you to forgive me. I accept that Jesus Christ died for me, was resurrected, and is alive today and hears my prayers. I now open my heart's door and invite You in to become my Lord and my Savior. I give you control and ask that you will rule and reign in my heart so that your perfect Will would be accomplished in my life. In Jesus name I pray, Amen.

After my family and I were saved we wanted to follow in water baptism. Acts 2:38 says, "Repent and be baptized, every one of you, in the name of Jesus Christ for the forgiveness of your sins. And you will receive the gift of the Holy Spirit." This scripture encourages us that when we are baptized, we are given the gift of the Holy Spirit and He becomes part of us. Water baptism does not save you; it is an act of faith and obedience to the commands of Christ. It declares that you are a follower of Jesus Christ. It is a public confession of your faith in Him.

So, we cannot earn salvation; we are simply saved by God's grace when we have faith in His Son, Jesus Christ. My prayer for you is that you will trust God as your personal Savior.

Chapter 2

Revelation

So here I am saved and born again at the age of 12. Little did my young heart know the transformation that would follow. 1 Corinthians 2:9 says, "No eye has seen, no ear has heard, and no mind has imagined what God has prepared for those who love Him." During my teen years I noticed my parents becoming more and more like Christ. My dad was a giver. He would give money to people in need and donate money to many ministries on television. I have seen him give cars away to people that could not afford a vehicle and even purchase transportation for church ministries. My mom was a prayer warrior. She would always post sticky notes with verses on mine and my brothers mirrors in our bedrooms for encouragement. She was loving, kind, and compassionate. Mom and dad both read their bibles, watched Christian television, along with attending church.

My mom instilled in me the importance of praying for my soulmate. She said that God had the perfect one picked out for me and would send him to me when the time was right. This is something she and I continually prayed about and looked forward to in the future. But, as I got older, it concerned me that I might not choose the right person. In fact, I needed God to write it in the sand or something. Maybe that's why I waited so late in life to get married. Time was moving quickly, and I was honestly afraid that I would end up like 'Delta Dawn'... "she's 41 and her daddy still calls her baby." Lol Well, at 28 years of age I truly believed that God sent me Mr. Right. We were married and a few years later had two beautiful daughters. Believe it or not I had never cooked a meal nor even washed a piece of clothing before getting married... I had so much to learn!

Through the years, life meant taking care of my daughters, parents, working late hours, and not spending quality time with my Mr. Right. Sadly, my parents were not doing well health wise and I became their caregiver along with working full time and taking care of my own family. In a way, maybe I put my own family's needs on the backburner, so to speak. But these were my parents, there isn't anything I wouldn't do for them, right? Many years later after my daughters were grown, one in college and the other in high school, things had changed tremendously. This particular night I was at a function at my youngest daughters' school. My emotions were a whirlwind because I knew I would be sitting alone again feeling insignificant and unworthy. Shouldn't I feel like a first lady? After all my Mr. Right was the Principal of the High School. Looking back, I remember going with him to try on several new suits for his first Administrative position. As he was being fitted for several new suits, I noticed how nice he looked and was extremely proud of him and all his accomplishments. This is what he had diligently worked for, and now God had opened a wonderful new door of opportunity for him and our family to walk through. I remember him telling me how distinguished it was to be a Head Administrator of a High School and just how prestigious it looked in the public eye. But in the midst of all the madness, somehow our family suffered. Instead of pulling together as a family should and keep God right smack in the center, we failed to nourish and care for one another and eventually we were torn apart.

As I sat on the bleachers alone watching my daughter having fun with her friends and loving her school, something unusual happened. It was as if I were watching a movie in slow motion as my Mr. Right began climbing up the bleachers as if he were going to sit with me for the very first time. For him to acknowledge me in public was so out of the ordinary. My eyes followed him as he made his way to the top and sat down next to me. Strangely enough, for one second, I felt a ray of hope for my marriage. But in my very next breath my heart sank as it sensed something tragically different.

In an instant I envisioned Jesus standing in the Garden of Gethsemane, patiently waiting for Judas to seal his own fate. Matthew 26:47-56 says, "And while He was still speaking, behold, Judas, one of the twelve, with a great multitude with swords and clubs, came from the chief priests and elders of the people. Now His betrayer had given them a sign, saying, "Whomever I kiss, He is the One; seize Him." Immediately he went up to Jesus and said, "Greetings, Rabbi:" and kissed Him. Judas betrayed Jesus with the kiss of death. And although on this night, I was not kissed, I knew the sting of betrayal, for I had felt it many times before. I began to realize that my betrayer had just given me a sign. And though my Mr. Right sat right next to me in the gym that night, we were a million miles apart. Just as Judas, was known as history's most famous traitor, he too would be remembered, by his family, in much the same way.

Chapter 3

Deserving

The fact of the matter is I did not feel worthy or good enough to ever be called a first lady. Maybe I had not worked on my credentials or bettered myself career wise, or maybe spent too much time working and taking care of others. Why, I spent over 25 years of marriage working and raising my daughters so that he could earn his degrees, military achievements, and follow his dreams, passions, and goals. How could my Mr. Right, have been so wrong? As I drove home alone, I wrestled with God. I don't know how I managed to stay on the road because I screamed and cried to the top of my lungs, tears everywhere! In fact, internally I was hoping that I would not survive this nightmare so that I would no longer experience this paralyzing pain ever again. I never knew that being so 'numb' could 'hurt' so bad.

God, I can't live this way anymore!

I am so miserable. My marriage is dead!

I can't take it anymore. I hate him!

I am so sick of all the lies of betrayal!

I hate what he has become and what he

has done to me! God, why did you allow this

to happen to me? Why would you even allow

me to marry him? I prayed my whole entire life

for you to send that perfect someone, and this is

what I get? I hate myself! I hate my life! I want out!

I want to die Lord!

Please save me!

I cannot remember a night that I didn't cry myself to sleep...and he never even knew. I felt nothing for so long... but I really wanted to.

Chapter 4

Steadfast

My marriage was destroyed, he was gone, and my daughters and I sat alone amidst the devastation. Painfully, this reminds me of chapter 1 of the book of Lamentations, Jeremiah mourns for Jerusalem and Judea as it lays in ruin by the raid and destruction of Babylon. Lamentations actually means the passionate expression of grief or sorrow; weeping. The name implies that the topic is expressing grief over something, to lament. In fact, Jeremiah is known as the "weeping prophet". He was an eyewitness and predicted this destruction, as did others, and this book sadly reflects on the devastation and immense suffering to his homeland. And as I lay in my marital wreckage, I realized that my entire world has just fallen apart. I didn't want a soul to know the truth. But how do you hide behind such grief? Surely death would be more bearable than the agony my heart sustained. I cried out...

God, I'm so old! Why did you let this happen?

I can't even support myself or my daughters!

Why are you punishing me, God? Where are you?

My life is over!

I'm better off dead than alive!

I had left everything that I had ever known to come to this new town and was even led to believe that things would get better… in some way or another. In fact, I also truly believed that God had already confirmed in my heart that this move was a part of His plan. I could have sworn I heard God correctly. How could I have been so wrong?

God, I am so stupid!

What on earth was I thinking?

Why God, why?

I gave it all up for this?

Why do you hate me God?

Why do you hate me?

This war cry was very familiar, as I had fought this battle many times before on my own. My wounded body was left for dead in the aftermath of what seemed like an attack from hell itself. My heart had been completely ripped out of my chest and exposed for all to see. Thinking I had just survived the most horrendous attack of my life, I was then hit with one more bombshell. The words, "We don't love each other and I'm just not happy", were the final blow. And as I lay there naked, afraid, and dying, somehow, I continued to live.

And like a caterpillar shedding its body for the last time, I had nothing left to give. Like a chrysalis, I just clung as

tightly as I could to my only Hope, the only One who could save me from this onslaught that I was in.
2 Corinthians 4:16-18 says, "Therefore we do not lose heart, but though our outer man is decaying, yet our inner man is being renewed day by day. For momentarily, these light afflictions are producing for you an eternal weight of glory, far beyond all comparison, as we look not at the things which are seen; for the things which are seen are temporal, but the things which are not seen are eternal."

"Light afflictions, God?" "What on earth?" It is important to understand that Jeremiah just saw his city fall to an invading army. He watched its gates burned to the ground and his family, friends, and neighbors killed. His whole world was falling apart and yet he wrote these encouraging words of hope through bitter tears. First, Jeremiah says, "I can't get these dreadful images out of my mind and they crush my heart. But even in my despair, I remember", "The steadfast love of the Lord never ceases; his mercies never come to an end; they are new every morning; great is your faithfulness. The Lord is my portion, says my soul, therefore I will hope in him." Lamentations 3:22-24

In plain English, you may be going through horrible circumstances and are facing dread, defeat, and unhappiness but God's mercies are like a relentless flood nothing can hold back. So, when you can't seem to hold on to anything else, please hold on to hope. Jeremiah's words are just as true in times of peace as in times of trouble. I also love Hebrews 10:23, "Let us hold firmly to the hope that we have confessed. We can trust God to do what He promised.

Chapter 5 

Where are you God?

Why don't you care about me?

I don't know what to do God!

I don't know where to go!

Can you even hear me God?

I need you!

Where are you God?

All my broken cries to God Almighty remind me so much of the disciples when they found themselves in a raging storm. It's found in Mark 4:38-40, I love the way The Message Bible reads, "As they were out on the water in a boat, a huge storm came up. Waves poured into the boat, threatening to sink it. And Jesus was in the stern, head on a pillow, sleeping! They roused him, saying,

Teacher, is it nothing to you that we're going down?

Do you not care if we perish?

We are going to drown!

Don't you care that we are about to die?

It is somewhat embarrassing to expose my mangled prayers in front of the world. But I believe it is super important that I am relatable to others. And I don't think for one moment that I am the only one who has felt this way. The truth is when the storms of life hit, and they will hit hard, you will get knocked down and sometimes angry with God because He seems nowhere to be found. You may lose your job and don't know how you can possibly pay your mortgage or continue to send your child to college. The doctor's diagnosis shows a raging disease that is taking over your body and there is no medical cure. You get a call from the hospital and your child has been involved in a serious automobile accident. Maybe you've been betrayed and abandoned, and your life has been turned upside down. Satan attacks minds during these treacherous times and tricks them into believing that God is not there and that He could not possibly care. When all the while as the storm is raging, He is just taking a nap in your boat.

Verses 39 and 40 of Mark say, "Awake now, He told the wind to pipe down and said to the sea, "Quiet! Settle down!" The wind ran out of breath; the sea became smooth as glass. Jesus reprimanded the disciples: "Why are you such cowards? Don't you have any faith at all?" Just know this, not only is Jesus in your boat, He wants you to ask Him to help you get through the storm. Great victory demands great defeat!

Even when I was at my weakest point wrestling with God and lashing out at Him, I knew deep down that God loved me and had not forgotten me. I just couldn't see Him, and I felt so alone, abandoned, and betrayed, probably much like you. One of the most encouraging verses I found during my greatest storm is Job 23:8-10 and it says, "Look, I go forward, but He is not there, and backward, but I cannot perceive Him; When He works on the left hand, I cannot behold Him; When He turns to the right hand, I cannot see Him." And here is the clincher, "but... He knows the way that I take; and when He has tested me, I shall come out as gold." One thing that I ultimately learned from the overwhelming waves of life is that even when things went wrong...it was right.

Chapter 6

Persevere

Sometimes we wear a smile to mask the suffering that we are so unpleasantly experiencing. It was a struggle to put on this intolerable facade that began to intensely cover and envelope me. I could barely take air into my lungs yet expel it. How could I pick myself up off the ground? How could I move on? The truth is... life goes on! Life goes on even after you have single-handedly destroyed every relationship that was important to you, after you've been fired, after your pet dies, after your child commits suicide, after your spouse leaves, after you've been injured and paralyzed. Life goes on! It goes on and on and on and on and on! You don't get to hit pause or take a break from living. There is no time to sit back and analyze the situation, no time to collect your thoughts. It won't wait for you. You must get up!!! Do not remain stagnant!

Believe me when I say life will hit you hard, and when it does, hit it back harder! Never forget that you have access to the 24/7 "Hotline to Heaven." "Be anxious for nothing, but in everything by prayer and supplication, with thanksgiving, let your requests be made known to God;

and the peace of God, which surpasses all understanding, will guard your hearts and minds through Christ Jesus." Philippians 4:6,7 So no matter how you fall, whether you simply fail God, or you get knocked down and brutally wounded by someone or circumstance, God is with you! "Yea, though I walk through the valley of the shadow of death, I will fear no evil; for You are with me; Your rod and Your staff, they comfort me." Psalm 23:4 No matter what hits you, knocks you down and shakes your world, stay focused on God and do not be afraid!

Proverbs 24:16 says, "For though the righteous fall seven times, and rise again, but the wicked stumble when calamity strikes." This verse speaks to God's faithfulness to His people who follow Him. The righteous are those who know the ways of God and keep them. The bible is full of promises for the righteous. God promises blessing beyond blessing for those who love Him and keep His commands. We are not promised a perfect and easy life if we follow Jesus and live according to His ways. For even when we fall into disbelief or failure at times, the Lord reaches out and picks us up. Consider Simon Peter, he fell many times. One example was when Peter got out of the boat and began walking on the water towards Jesus. In Matt 14:30 it says, "But seeing the wind, he became frightened, and beginning to sink, he cried out "Lord, save me"! Peter took his eye off the Lord and focused them on the raging sea and immediately the next verse tells us, "Jesus stretched out His hand and took hold of him." Peter fell and immediately the Lord picked him up. Peter's greatest fall is recorded in Matthew 26:69-74, where Peter denied the Lord three times. It says, "And Peter remembered the words which Jesus had said, "Before a rooster crows, you will deny Me three times." And he went out and wept bitterly. Again, Peter fell, and the Lord picked him up.

One moment, I too would be focused on God feeling as if I could conquer the world and walk on water, and in the next moment find myself gasping for breath, drowning out in the deep end. My cries out to God tasted so bitter and fear tormented my soul. This would all seem too much to bear!

Where are you God?

I don't know what to do!

I have nowhere to live!

I need a job with benefits, God!

Do you not care?

I need help God!

My daughters need help!

Where are you God?

Please save us Lord!

And of course, God picked me up and saved me and my daughters again and again and again. He will pick you up too! Your fall may look different than that of mine, Peter, Job, Jeremiah, Paul, and many others. But God promises that even if we fail God or get knocked down to the ground for whatever reason, we will rise again.

We know that we are shaped and refined by trial and testing, so not only do we accept it, but we also thank God for anything that helps us to grow in our likeness of Him. Sometimes difficult times must happen for God to accomplish His purpose in our lives. "For I know the thoughts that I think toward you, says the Lord, thoughts of peace and not of evil, to give you a future and hope." Jeremiah 29:11

And as resilient as the righteous of Christ are, the unrighteous are fragile. When "calamity strikes" they will stumble and fall into tribulation and distress and have no Divine Resources to help them. So please take comfort in knowing that God never makes a mistake and He knows what is best. When life hits you hard remember, you are stronger than you think. "I can do all things through Christ who strengthens me." Philippians 4:13

That night as I walked through the doorway of the banquet room filled with family and friends, not a soul knew the internal injury my body held deep within. I only remember one statement made on this night of my grandmother's 97th birthday celebration. Her brother, my great Uncle Ed, when asked, what advice he could give to all of us after living such a long and happy life said, "Keep a smile on your face, a song in your heart, and peace in your soul." So, that's exactly what I did.

Chapter 7 

Fervent

I remember my situation seeming so hopeless and impossible. I had no strength to even face the numerous trials my daughters and I would encounter. And of course, when it rains, it pours, right? Sadly, not knowing how I would possibly get my daughter to school, how I could pay bills with my income, or get the grass cut which was knee high, were really the least of my worries. Desperately I sought God on my hands and knees fervently in prayer. And...when I didn't know what to pray or even how to pray, I would write down prayers that I found online and critically cry them out!

You are my strength when I am weak.

You are my rock when I am slipping.

You are my deliverer when I am trapped.

You are my fortress when I am crumbling.

You are my refuge when I am pursued.

You are my shield when I am exposed.

You are my Lord when my life spins out of control!

And boy, was my life out of control! Immediately my need for transportation to get my daughter to and from school was met. Praise God! She was given a vehicle and it was almost as if I threw her out to the wolves, on Highway 82, one of my biggest fears. I learned rather quickly to trust God with an exclamation point! The pressure to make a mortgage payment, school athletic fees, and continue to support my oldest in college seemed to be more than my mental, physical, and emotional state could manage.

I remember walking into my church, Journey Church of the River Region, in Prattville, that first Sunday so broken and frail hoping no one would notice. I saw a pamphlet for prayer requests located on the back-seat pocket of the chair in front of me that could be filled out and put in the offering bag. Sunday after Sunday inconspicuously, I would sneak a brochure and begin writing my many prayer requests down and put them in the bag at the end of the service. I recall even writing an apology note for using most of the leaflets. Lol As my daughters and I were quickly trying to get out of that first service without any confrontations, it happened. God sent someone up to me and they prayed for me and my family. Not only that, but God also sent a Christian Counselor my way to encourage, give hope, and provide spiritual support during my most trying time. It was so encouraging to know that not only God had my back, but so did my church family. They continually prayed over all my many prayer request brochures from week to week. Funny now, but I was probably known as the River Region prayer request 'brochure burglar'! lol And I say this, only, because I believe it is extremely important, and that is I continued to tithe, even when I didn't have the money to do so. I have always been taught the significance of giving God what is rightfully His and I honestly believe, because of this, I am abundantly blessed.

Someone encouraged me to watch the movie, "War Room", which is about a family whose lives take an unexpected turn. They are inspired by a prayer warrior who encourages them to find happiness through prayer. My favorite quote from this movie was a prayer that the main character prayed. She said, "Lord, help him love me again, and help me love him again." This movie incredibly changed my life and this prayer became a major part of my life. I was determined to make myself a War Room. I immediately began taping verses all over my closet. I would teach early morning online classes with my Chinese students and then run as fast as I could to my War Room and hit the ground just weeping and weeping and weeping. I tried so hard to encourage myself like David did in the bible. I would shout out....

Whatever is true.

Whatever is noble.

Whatever is right.

Whatever is pure.

Whatever is lovely.

Whatever is admirable.

If anything is excellent or praiseworthy

think about such things.

And…

I am loved.

I am wonderful.

I am beautiful.

I have a purpose.

I am a masterpiece.

God has a great plan for me.

In 1 Samuel 30:1-6, David is a great example of how to respond to discouragement. The Amalekites had made a raid on Ziklag and burned it with fire; and they took the women and children captive. When King David and his men arrived, everyone was grieved over the situation and wept. The people appeared to have blamed David for the tragedy and wanted to stone him. He was greatly distressed, for all the people were embittered, each one because of his sons and his daughters. But David strengthened himself in the Lord his God…meaning – he encouraged himself through prayer and trusting God, remembering God's past deliveries and believing that God is in control.

David writes, and it's worth repeating, "Even though I walk through the valley of the shadow of death, I fear no evil, for You are with me; Your rod and your staff, they comfort me." What better author to write a psalm on God's provisions than King David, who once was a shepherd himself? Sometimes the "Valley of the shadow of death" can appear to be a terminal disease, abuse from a family member, separation or divorce, a horrible financial circumstance, betrayal of a friend, death of a loved one. Whatever your valley may be, God says to trust Him. He will walk with you so do not fear. It's important that we do not *only* rely on others for comfort and support but encourage ourselves with the Word of God.

Of course, I did have a few people who were voices of inspiration. One day God had my very special friend Cricket call me at what seemed like... in the nick of time, to shower me with uplifting words. I continued to receive texts from her periodically that would truly give me the extra strength needed to push through. I reconnected with a sweet military friend, Sabrina, who prayed for me and sent me encouraging words and sermons to listen to. I really don't know what I would have done without my brother David and best friend Anji. They stayed close by my side through thick and thin as I regurgitated all my emotions, good and bad on them at all hours of the day and night. In fact, my whole family had to endure the repercussion of my brokenness. I couldn't have survived without all of them, especially my brothers, Danny and David.

My emotions were crazy, as if I were on a rollercoaster. I would be praising God like I was on top of the world and in the very next breath fall to the ground in a fetal position begging God to kill me. Satan had a tight grip on my emotions, and I was led to believe that my children would be better off, if I were dead. You see I had no job security, no benefits, no nothing. I couldn't support myself, much less my daughters. I felt too old to start over, but I had no choice. My car was on the blink and my tire was flat, my younger daughter's car engine blew up, my oldest daughter had a tire blowout on a bridge. I had a benign lipoma removed from my arm that took months to heal, and a mass had been found in my uterus. All of this within a couple of months along with trying to find a place to live and taking care of my dad who was in very bad health, all at the same time. In my exhaustion from earthly struggles, many times, I would find myself walking down the hill to my next-door neighbor Kristen's house, to sit on her couch and just cry.

Chapter 8

Transfiguration

The change that occurs in a caterpillar inside the chrysalis is slow and gradual. In fact, the caterpillar's body digests itself from the inside out. This creature is attacked by the same sort of juices that it used in its earlier life to digest food. Many of the organs are hidden in the caterpillar and they take a new form within the chrysalis. You see, the old body is broken down into imaginal cells but not all the tissues are destroyed. Some tissues pass onto the insect's new body. One imaginal disk will become a wing and there are imaginal disks that form the legs, antennae and the other organs of the butterfly.

Like the caterpillar, many times, our bodies are broken down and need rebuilding. Hosea 6:1 says, "Come let us return to the Lord; for He has torn us, that He may heal us; He has struck us down, and He will bind us up." This process can sometimes take a long time and it is extremely important that we continue to hold on tightly to God's promises. In my case I suffered personal rejection, several times, that truly left scars on my soul. My frail body suffered tremendously and was extremely thin. I would literally force myself to eat so that I could live. One of my many prayers was that I wouldn't lose my hair as I had once before in the past. I fasted and prayed, fasted and prayed, fasted and prayed for my family. I would walk and pray, walk and pray, walk and pray for a miracle. I remember walking everyday along a path filled with many weeping willows and God just reaching down from heaven and drying every tear that flowed from my face. I did not want this rejection to embitter my mind and rob me of joy and peace for the rest of my life. Although my family was destroyed, I wanted to run out of the prison of resentment quickly and recapture Gods everlasting love.

It is so true that destruction comes before our reconstruction. In Ephesians 4:20 -24 the apostle says, "We were taught to put off our old selves which belongs to our former manner of life and is corrupt through deceitful desires and to be renewed in the spirit of our minds." Cancer may show up on a routine doctor's visit. Or a spouse leaves and abandons their family. An unexpected loss of a loved one, or you are overcome with boundless depression. Being broken down and needing rebuilding is when you thought you were going to do great things for God, or have a great family, or have a successful career, and it becomes clear that things are not working out the way you dreamed of. Or in fact, the rug gets pulled out from under you and your life becomes torn apart. An unknown poet once said, it is the place where you are, "pressed into knowing no helper but God."

I will always remember how nervous I was to go to school and watch my daughter in all of her extracurricular activities. I felt a sense of being unwanted and allowed my emotions to get the best of me. I felt unworthy, insignificant, unloved, a failure, embarrassed, humiliated, foolish, and much more. God knew I needed this particular person at this particular time in my life. And whether she walked in the gym, football stadium, softball field, you name it, she would intentionally find me and sit with me. Michelle's presence did my heart so good. Natasha, another wonderful friend would allow me to ride with her or follow her to all the games. And one time after my dad had passed, I was really at my wits end, Shelly hugged my neck and said a little prayer in my ear. I am forever grateful for all the Coaches, teachers, and friends from BHS, who never failed to lend PresLee a helping hand, offer her words of encouragement and prayers, and give her tender hugs and smiles.

My oldest daughter HeartLee was away at college, living with my dad, so I had a sense of peace knowing that she was lovingly being taken care of. But little did I know that would not last for long. After my dad's passing, my daughter's boyfriend, Cole and his family reached out in so many ways to not only help my daughter but help me also. We are forever grateful.

There were many moments when I honestly just needed to receive a 'text' from God Himself...and He never failed me. My phone would 'ding' and my sweet cousin

Leslie, always had the perfect verse or Word from God that really hit the spot. Her sister, Sheri had a prayer request white board in her dining room and added my family to it. She said every time she walked by it, she lifted us up in prayer. A few close friends at work continued giving me encouragement and my sweet friend Liz, whom I greatly admire, always sent me verses and inspirational devotions during the day.

I spent countless hours on my knees before God Almighty praying that He would open a door for me to have a job with wonderful benefits, I needed a new car and a home. When it seems, your world is tumbling down, sometimes life becomes 'all about me'. During this season I was so wrapped up in *my* hurt and in *my* pain. I felt the need to find answers. Looking through old bills, credit cards, and social media became my daily routine. And with every tidbit of information I could gather, or pictures I would find, would initially be like me injecting myself with a deadly poison but not dying. Why would anyone want to continually torture themselves in this way? *Me, me, me, me, me, me, me, me*! When I was at my lowest, I was definitely at my most *selfish* state.

This is not who I wanted to be, and I did not want divorce to be a part of my story. So, I began to pray, "Please God change me, change me, change me, change me, change me." I posted prayers for each member of my family and friends on my War Room wall and tried to focus my eyes on God. I began thanking God for what I had instead of what I had lost. I had lists of people dangling from my closet that I continually prayed for, many of whom have no idea to this day that they were ever even lifted up in prayer.

My dad was my hero and I hated to see him in the condition that he was in. His heart was deteriorating and becoming very weak, which led him to believe that he did not have much more time here on earth with his family. His anxiety grew and I believe he was afraid of dying alone. I wanted him to come and live with me, but he just could not feel comfortable in someone else's house. He wanted to be in his own home and be able to attend his own church and be near his own friends. I prayed continually that God would take away all the fear he was facing and the anxiety he was suffering and give him joy, peace, and good health for the rest of his time here on earth. And boy did I need my dad here on earth at this time! You see, I was daddy's little girl and he was concerned for me too. For years I had become so dependent on others as if I were incapable of doing anything on my own. Sadly, when I lost my dad, I learned what it meant to become utterly dependent upon God. The last three months of my dad's life here on earth were lived in peace, joy, with no fear of the future. How amazing God is, definitely an answer to my many prayers. And as my brothers, sister-n-law, and I gathered around my dad in the hospital room that sorrowful morning, I could sense God's Presence. With worship music silencing some of the pain pounding at our hearts, we prayed as God welcomed my dad in His arms. I so wanted to keep my dad forever, but God had something far greater in store.

My Dad - My Hero

Daniel Robert Long Sr

Chapter 9

Faithfulness

Oh, how I wanted restoration for my family! It was extremely important to me that my daughters see a miracle of God happen before their very own eyes. But there seemed to be no hope in all the debris. In the book of Nehemiah, we read that the Jews were in a similar predicament. Life had taken them by surprise; they had been attacked, taken captive, and had lost their homes and were discouraged. They were disgraced and there was no plan to repair their city for safety and for dignity. Maybe you can relate? Have you ever felt like the people of Israel? Is life overwhelming and unbearable? God used Nehemiah in a significant way to bring God's people together to rebuild and restore the city of Jerusalem.

God miraculously used the hopeless to accomplish a great work. You may find yourself in a similar situation where you have a sense of hopelessness, tragedy, and heartache. Are you willing to allow God to pick up all the pieces and rebuild your life? God was faithful then and He is still faithful today. The Jews needed a new perspective and a new start to rebuild not only their homes, but also their lives. Nehemiah stood in the gap and interceded on their behalf. He led a group of Jews to Jerusalem in order to rebuild the city walls. In fact, it says in Nehemiah 6:16 that "On the twenty-fifth day of the month Elul, the wall was completely rebuilt. It had taken fifty-two days." It happened to them, and it can happen to you, too! God can definitely bring beauty out of brokenness!

I began to see the manifestation of my prayers in full bloom. I am so very thankful for the many blessings and favor God showered on me and my daughters during the most difficult time of our lives. God provided a way when there seemed to be no way. He opened a door for me not only to get a new car but a home close to my daughters' school, for her senior year. Praise God for answered prayers! That is just how good He is! It didn't happen overnight though; in fact, it took a year of praying and believing before I was able to get a car, and a house, and fifteen months for the job with benefits to open up. There were times I really didn't know how I would be able to afford food for my daughters and pets, and gas, much less be able to save any money, especially for emergency situations. And of course, the devil held nothing back. He would aim and fire, aim and fire, aim and fire! An unexpected bill out of nowhere suddenly appeared, and the septic tank and air conditioner both took a dive for the worst. Water ankle deep in all the tubs and sinks, were only a few of my concerns. Instead of cursing God and dying, I simply laid it at God's feet, and He provided help.

I want to reiterate how I spent many months praying, fasting, and looking for a house, interviewing for jobs and trusting God for His perfect timing.... not so easy! Belief, unbelief, belief, unbelief, belief, unbelief, belief and unbelief! I would cry out, Mark 9:24 over and over and over. It says, "Lord, I believe; but help my unbelief", "Lord, I believe; but help my unbelief", "Lord, I believe; but help my unbelief! "I know you've been there too!

We learn in Romans 8:28 that God is faithful. He will reveal His work in His own timing and take care of you in the 'mean time'! The time I am talking about here is God's timing not our timing because God's timing, scripture tells us, is perfect. Rest in God, while He is working behind the scenes and not striving to make things happen in our own strength. You see God had been rearranging everything for our good, even when it did not feel so good, even in the tough times.

Chapter 10

Gratefulness

Although God never left my side, I struggled with unanswered questions and unanswered prayer. Guilt, impatience, unforgiveness, resentment, remorse, continually flooded my soul. The truth is... life is hard! But in my mind and heart I just couldn't fathom how someone could betray and abandon their family without a sign of remorse or regret whatsoever. How could someone so easily and quickly walk out, and never look back. How do you do that?

I blame myself for not being the kind of wife that I should have been. I am showered with so many regrets. And oh, the many thoughts, emotions, and visions that continually tormented my heart, mind, and soul. Boy, was I grateful that God sent a special friend named Derek my way to teach me an awesome prayer to pray whenever my emotions would get the best of me. He told me to raise my hands high up in the air and say..." Jesus, please take this emotion from my soul. Jesus, please heal my soul. Jesus, thank you for my healing." I must have prayed this prayer a hundred times a day for many months, and sometimes I still do. Funny, I remember one day while driving down the road, I was having a bit of a "Why, God, why", kinda day, so I lifted my hands in the air. I said,"Jesus, please take this emotion from my soul. Jesus, please heal my soul. Jesus, I accept Your healing." When suddenly I heard a beeping sound from the dashboard of my car and saw the words…." Please keep your hands on the steering wheel." lol True story. I have now learned to let Jesus take the wheel!

I had become a prayer warrior and saw prayers answered daily one by one. Yes, many answered prayers…. all except for one. I begged God to give me signs that restoration was at hand, and He did, however metamorphosis had only begun, and I knew the break of me would be the make of me. My daughters and I continued to struggle financially, and I was told that my lawyer could enforce financial help if I filed for the big D. Of course, this is not what I wanted or intended to do, but after many months of prayer and consideration I believed it was necessary, so sadly I did. But month after month, prayer after prayer, there were still no signs of help, but God taught me one of the biggest lessons from this critical situation. I learned to be utterly dependent only on God and no one else…. ever!

In fact, I love, love, love, the way The Message Bible interprets Philippians 4:19. It says, "And now I have it all-and keep getting more! The gifts you sent with Epaphroditus were more than enough, like a sweet-smelling sacrifice roasting on the altar, filling the air with fragrance, pleasing God to no end."

You can be sure that God will take care of everything you need, His generosity exceeding even yours in the glory that pours from Jesus. Our God and Father abounds in glory that just pours out into eternity. Yes! He supplies all our needs!!! So, I just laid all my needs at His feet... and let it go.

Chapter 11 

Faith

In order to be able to become a butterfly, the caterpillar must fall apart completely, decompose down to its very essence, devoid of any shape or consciousness. It literally dies. There is nothing left of it. This transitional season was long and treacherous, and my hearts cry became, "God, please intervene in 2019! And the pain I saw in both my daughter's eyes brought double anguish. I knew that God could snap His fingers and in two seconds this turning of my family inside out would be over. But If we were to bypass the wilderness journey, then we would bypass open heart surgery! There truly needed to be a death experience before a resurrection could occur. Jesus isn't revealed in our easy...He is revealed in our storm! It is in the storm when our faith is greatly tested.

A good example of faith is found in the story of the Battle of Jericho. God instructed Joshua to have his army walk around the walls of Jericho once a day for six straight days. While marching the soldiers played their trumpets as the priests carried the Ark of the Covenant around the city of Jericho. On the seventh day the Israelites marched around the city of Jericho seven times. At Joshua's order, the men produced a powerful roar, and Jericho's walls miraculously fell down. The Israelite army raced in quickly conquering the city. This is found in Joshua 6:2-5. Think about this, if a portion of the walls of Jericho had fallen each day, the children of Israel would not have needed to trust God with the end result.

Faith over fear, faith over fear, faith over fear! You see, I was holding on to faith for the restoration of my family when in fact, I feared God was not finished with me yet. Could it have been me He was waiting on? Rejection is the sense of being unwanted which left a deep wound on my soul and robbed me of my joy. You may be recovering from rejection too. Whether your mother never showed you love, you never even knew your dad, your employer overlooked you for the promotion, or possibly you were abandoned at birth, its plain and simple....rejection hurts! Rejection can lead to a downward spiral of negative introspection and an overall sense of not feeling "good enough." Not only did I not feel "good enough", I had no more hopes, dreams, or desires left in me. In a way, I believe that I was in the dying phase of the caterpillar transformation, nothing left.

But what kept me going was a sure reminder from God Himself. It went something like this, "Those who wait on the Lord – I promise I will renew your strength. And when you think you can't take one more breath...I'll give you enough to keep going on, and keep going on, and enough to keep going on, and to keep going on. Strength will rise in you when you keep going on. And you will feel like you have been swept up on wings as eagles. You will run and not get weary and walk and not faint. I will hold you, even when you let go of me. I'm not going to let go of you." And this is found in Isaiah 40:31.

But you know what? God has the final word about what is going to happen in my marriage, and what's going to happen with your health, and what's going to happen with our children, and what's going to happen with your life. Jeremiah 33:3 says, "You pray child of God, call upon me, and I will answer you and show you great and mighty things." God's way is perfect. We may not understand His plans, but we can trust it to be better than anything we could devise for ourselves! Here is a simple prayer for the not so simple moments.

Father, I declare that You are good! You can be trusted! Help me trade my unbelief for the beautiful relief that I don't have to figure everything out. I just have to fix my eyes and thoughts on you Jesus and how You will lead me. I don't have to understand...I just have to trust! In Jesus name, Amen!

Your situation may look hopeless, it may seem like it's the end, but God is your ever-present help In time of need. Trust Him to give you the grace and strength to make it through every trial.

Chapter 12

Beautiful

I love the way The Message Bible depicts the story of Mary and Martha. In Luke 10:38-42, it says, “As they continued their travel, Jesus entered a village. A woman by the name of Martha welcomed him and made him feel quite at home. She had a sister, Mary, who sat before the Master, hanging on every word he said. But Martha was pulled away by all she had to do in the kitchen. Later, she stepped in, interrupting them. “Master, don’t you care that my sister has abandoned the kitchen to me? Tell her to lend me a hand.” The Master said, “Martha, dear Martha, you’re fussing far too much and getting yourself worked up over nothing. One thing only is essential, and Mary has chosen it- it’s the main course and won’t be taken from her.”

I believe the story of Mary and Martha is truly about prioritizing the Word of God in our daily walk with Him. In fact, the teachings of Jesus were dramatically actualized in both women’s lives. They are women of excellence and noble character. I just couldn’t fathom though how Mary could so nonchalantly just sit still and not help her sister. Yes, I took up for Martha for many years, in fact, I was

Martha. I loved Christ and longed to spend more time with Him, but I let the distractions of life overwhelm me. Like Martha, I allowed the preparations of serving and focusing on all the details get in my way and at times felt choked by worries and cares of life. Martha wanted to please Jesus and show love by being hospitable and making Him feel welcome. Mary, on the other hand, did not sit beside Jesus, a place of honor, but at His feet, a place of humility. Mary shows her love by sitting at Jesus' feet soaking in every word that He uttered. She did not want to miss a second of His teachings and stories. Mary sits and takes it all in like a sponge, she can't imagine anything better than this!

I mention this story because when things come crashing down in life, or do not turn out as planned, or you hit rock bottom, in a manner of speaking, there is no place better to be than at Jesus' feet. And I strongly urge you to not wait for something traumatic to happen before developing an intimate relationship with God. After all these years I finally understand Mary's heart. You see, no other feet in the entire world were more beautiful to Mary than the feet of Jesus. And just as Jesus had changed her life, He had changed mine. It took many years for me to develop a heart like Mary, but now spending time with God is not only an essential part of my Christian life, but it is top priority. I can't imagine letting a second go by without spending time with my Father God each day. In fact, I can't face life without Him, don't want to. There is nothing better than resting in His presence, reading His word and speaking to Him in prayer, and there is no place I would rather be.

It has been more than two years and I haven't turned on the television to watch a program other than a Christian station. I long to constantly listen to preachers and motivational speakers on YouTube as I get ready in the mornings and on my drive to work. I read many devotions throughout the week and post Christlike inspirations on Social Media. Like Martha, I have a longing to serve others and be an encourager. But like Mary, I can't get enough of God poured into my life. And I want more of Him...nothing else is satisfying. And I say this not to boast, but because I am ever so grateful how far God has brought me. He loves me unconditionally and will never leave or abandon me. When everyone else walks away...He stays! So, if you look for me and cannot find me.... just know, I'll be at Jesus' feet.

Chapter 13 

Prayer

The holidays were here yet again, which were altogether extremely challenging not only for me but my daughters as well. During these difficult times I would ask God to please open my eyes so that I could see what He was doing. But I had comfort in knowing that though I couldn't see Gods hands.... I could trust His heart. God blessed me with a new job that had excellent benefits and allowed me to continue teaching my ESL classes in China online. I was thankful that I could continue teaching my students but was concerned about their health due to the virus in China. My students occasionally wore masks and spoke of it often and I could tell that they were concerned too. My precious student Elaine, who is five years old told me that she had a swimming pool in her backyard. When asked if she enjoyed swimming in her pool, she responded, "Only when there is no Corona Virus in the water." She speaks English very well. My students and their parents were concerned about me too. One mother mentioned that I looked very thin and she was worried about me. Remember, I was going through a transformation which affected me not only emotionally but physically as well, my self-esteem vanished. One night before opening my computer camera to teach, I heard my student guo guo practicing with his dad what he would say to me during class. He said, "Teacher Daun, you are beautiful in my heart." So sweet, tears! On Valentine's day I woke up to a trail of sticky notes all over the house with affirmations on them from my daughter. "You are beautiful, you are enough, you are worth it, you are strong, you are loved, you are kind, you are funny, you are talented, you are healed, you are smart, you are giving, and so many more....still have each note. Both my daughters presented me with a beautiful ring, engraved with their names and We love you Momma, on it, that I will always cherish.

God sent my friend and coworker, Julie into my life who helped open the door for me to have this new job. She had much more confidence in me than I could have ever conjured up. I absolutely loved my new job, and all of my coworkers were friendly and made me feel welcomed. However, I had never had a job quite like this before and didn't know if I was capable of doing it. I would work 8-5, jump in my car and cry all the way home, then teach my Chinese students. I cried not only because I couldn't get the hang of this new office job, but because I just couldn't figure out God's plan for my life. I taught school for 30 years and could put on programs and productions literally blindfolded with hundreds of students alone, but to answer a phone and transfer it to the precise department seemed inconceivable. I had the best teacher, Stephany to prepare me for this job and am so grateful for her patience, but each day I was like the little piggy that went wah, wah, wah, all the way home! I would pray and ask God to help me because I didn't want to get fired. Finally, one day, believe it or not, I was driving home on the interstate, cars flying by me on both sides, and beeping me off the road. No one would allow me to maneuver my car into the correct lane in order to take my exit. Instead of panicking, I simply just took a deep breath, had no worries, and got off on the wrong exit. Guess what? No tears! Yay! I am so very grateful for Vickie, Mr. Strickland and all my coworkers for taking me under their wings, believing in me, and giving me an opportunity to work with a wonderful company that truly feels like family. Boy did this job do my heart good.

God most certainly was taking me in a new life direction. I began praying that God would give me hopes, dreams, goals, and visions that had somehow gotten lost along the way. My coworker Tamekia had written a book and had placed several copies in the breakroom. This inspired me to finish writing a book I began several years ago. During my breaks and lunch hour at work every day, I would walk and talk with God. I remember walking outside one morning to spend time in prayer and I took a deep, long breath. Immediately I knew that I was going to make it through this tough season and that God was in the process of healing my life. At this moment I knew that what Jesus did for me was so much greater than what someone else had done to me. I had hope...and hope felt good.

I began reading inspirational books constantly and listening to preachers and speakers online. There were actually three renown women of God who I lived off of and who helped me to keep pushing through the most difficult times, Autumn Miles, Real Talk Kim, and Karen Wheaton…don't know what I would have done without them. A coworker and friend, Julia, invited me to a banquet at her church. The title of the message was, "leaving room at the table for someone." I felt God really impress upon my heart to think of others more than I do myself and have a servant's heart. My brother had already been telling me for months to find people to serve, so I made an effort each day to find someone to serve and also asked God to send people my way.

Although I had become a prayer warrior, sometimes I had no words left in me. I began to look up prayers online and make copies for myself. While on my lunch break one afternoon, I laid a stack of prayers on my desk and my coworker and sweet friend, Kitoria asked me if I would make her some prayers too. Of course, I did, but didn't want to hand her a bunch of prayers that could easily scatter. So, I punched a whole through each prayer, made a cover, then connected them with a big hoop earring. She loved it and told me several friends wanted what they called "A Ring of Prayers". So, there you have it, they gave my vision a name and God gets the glory. I have enjoyed making many prayer rings and feel honored to share them with others.

During this somewhat new season of my life God also gave me the desire to post inspirational stories and devotions on Social Media. I never even knew if anyone ever really paid any attention to the devotions that I felt were truly inspired by God. One day at work, Rob a coworker, mentioned that he was having a rough week and he came across my devotion and it really ministered to his heart! Wow! Praise God! I thought if God could touch a man through my devotions, then He most certainly can touch others also. This really lifted my spirit and confidence level.

I had somehow managed to read about 15 inspirational books and wanted to share them with others but was not quite sure how to go about it. One night as I lay in bed, I could not sleep. I felt God putting into my spirit a sort of book club vision. Immediately I thought of R&R which not only stands for rest and relaxation, but in my case, Read and Render. Read and Render became the name of my newly named book club. This is the gist of it, I would read a book and freely give it to someone else filled with homemade surprises like bookmarkers, verses, prayers etc. The only stipulation was that I asked once they finished reading the book that they freely render it to someone else. This way we could spread Gods love all over the state of Alabama and possibly around the world. Even still, I continue to read, and it does my heart good to freely render to the next person. I even have friends rendering their books too.

Isn't God good? God has given me the opportunity to sing on my church worship team for the last two years and I have already written two books. I say this only to encourage you to allow God to pour dreams, goals, and visions into your soul that you once had or never even dreamed of. He is a God of second chances, and it is never too late!

Me

Photo by: Hunter Heath

Chapter 14

Forgiveness

During this transformation process, we must allow the old world inside of us, our habits, beliefs, our fears and footholds, to die and disintegrate. It is a little scary and really has nothing to do with a cozy nap inside a soft time capsule. It's really about surrendering yourself to the darkness, completely letting go and letting God put you back together again. Many times, we say we want to change, but conveniently forget there is a necessary process to endure in order to emerge transformed. Unfortunately, we cannot bypass the different and somewhat difficult stages of transformation.

God continued to give me wisdom and insight about many things, especially about walking by faith and not by sight. Every day I continually repeated, "I walk by faith and not by sight, I walk by faith and not by sight, I walk by faith and not by sight". I was extremely honored to be asked by my dear friend, Shannon, to be a breakout leader at a women's convention at church, but little did I know that the conference would touch on a topic that I was not so familiar with, forgiveness. I was a little at war with myself when it came to this subject. You see, I really wanted to forgive, but really wasn't sure if I could or even how to go about doing it. During my prayer time, I would cry out, "I forgive, I forgive, please God, help me to forgive. I would tell anyone who knew my situation that I was devastated but not destroyed and I was better, but not bitter! But was I? How could I be sure? And how could I possibly teach about forgiveness when I wasn't sure if I even knew what forgiveness was.

So, while preparing for my breakout session, I asked God to show me what forgiveness looked like. It was as if He immediately whispered in my ear the words, "to wish well". I had never thought of it this way, and it seemed super easy. Really? No, on the contrary, it was super difficult. But I didn't want to be bound in chains of unforgiveness the rest of my life, I longed for freedom, and the ability to one day soar like a butterfly high in the sky, to endless heights. So I began to cry out..."I wish him well, I wish her well, I wish them well, I wish him well, I wish her well, I wish them well, I wish him well, I wish her well, I wish them well." My goal was to pray this prayer continually over and over and over until one day I would sincerely and totally have forgiven completely. In my desperation I began praying another prayer that I learned. I would call each name out loud... You can add your own names.

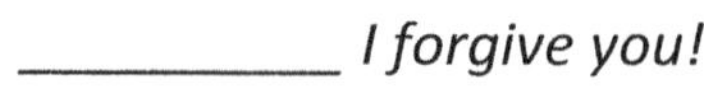

I choose in my heart to forgive you!

I will in my heart to forgive you!

You are free to go!

You are free to leave my hurt and my pain!

God, because you tell me to do it as an act of my will,

I choose to forgive them!

____________ *you are free to leave the prison of my anger!*

_____________ *you are free to leave the prison of my pain!*

I drop the charges against you!

I choose to release you!

I did the best that I could and asked God to do what I couldn't. My daughters and I faced some extremely difficult times financially and emotionally. Not only was I struggling to keep my head above water, I was trying to hold both my daughters up at the same time so they wouldn't drown either. And like the Titanic, we were turning upside down, exhausted and sinking! When your children are hurt, prayers don't always sound hunky dory. During one of those hits from Satan, one of my lowest moments, I recall crying out...

Today, I do not wish him well!

No, in fact, I wish him all the many devastating emotions

that he caused in mine and my daughters' lives!

I wish him pain, sorrow, embarrassment,

humiliation, suffering, loss of appetite, troubles,

nightmares, sleeplessness, no one to turn to, regret,

shame, depression, misery, hurt, no peace, severe sadness, a broken heart, and loneliness! I forgive him only because God tells me to, and I will forgive him all day, every day until I don't have to forgive him anymore, which means, I finally forgive him! But I do not wish him well today, and

maybe not tomorrow or the next day either.

But...I will forgive him no matter how long it takes!

Then maybe, I can wish him well again...

I only allow you to see some of the ugly... because devastating times are not always pretty. You know, you've been there before, too. Our emotions do not tell us the truth about forgiveness. It does not depend on how we feel, for Satan enjoys stirring up emotions. And on this day my emotions were at their wits end. Gratefully, my friend Sharon Fortune posted this verse on my FB page which said, "I keep my eyes always on the Lord. With Him at my right hand, I will not be shaken." Psalm 16:8,9

You see, I did not have my eyes on God, but on man and I was definitely shaken. Now, I realize the importance of keeping my eyes focused on Him and not on people and circumstances around me. Time and time again, God's people hurt each other and hurt Him. Yet God forgave them every time they turned to Him. Forgiveness is what God does when He marks "cancelled" over our debt of sin, when He declares us legally acquitted, regardless of how we might be feeling at the moment. Matthew 6:14-15 says, "If you forgive other people when they sin against you, your heavenly Father will also forgive you. But if you do not forgive others their sins, your Father will not forgive your sins." Jesus teaches His disciples in Luke 17:4 that they are to forgive "seventy-seven times" or over and over again. Just like His forgiveness doesn't run out, neither should ours.

A perfect example of forgiveness is found in Gen 50:15-21. It is about Joseph and his jealous brothers throwing him into a well, left for dead, then selling him to passing slave-traders and reporting his 'death' to their father. He eventually was wrongly accused by Potiphar's wife while working in the palace and thrown into prison for a long time. Years later Joseph interpreted a dream for Pharaoh by which he found favor and power in Egypt. Robbed of those precious years by the betrayal of his own brothers, if anyone had just cause to bear a grudge, Joseph did. The story continues with a severe famine in the Middle East which drives Joseph's brothers to Egypt in search of grain to purchase. Joseph has compassion on them, giving them grain and finally revealing himself to them and bringing the whole family to live in Egypt. The brothers showed more anxiety for their future than genuine sorrow for their past actions. Joseph forgave his brothers despite their poor confession.

But, confession, like the original wrong done to us, is an action of the other person and as such we cannot control it. Forgiveness is something which God commands us to do, an action that I may choose, and which is not dependent upon the behavior of the other person. He commands it for our own good and for the good of the other person as well. In other words, I forgive no matter what! Joseph's brothers were not really coming clean with him and he probably suspected this, but Joseph forgave them anyway. Forgiving is not excusing or forgetting the behavior of another person. In fact, Joseph said it best to his brothers in Genesis 50:20, "You intended to harm me, but God intended it for good to accomplish what is now being done, the saving of many lives".

And I feel this so true in my own life as well. It took me quite some time to realize that forgiveness is incomplete until love replaces anger, not easy but possible with God. And just as Joseph was no longer led by anger, and able to wish his brothers well, I wanted my daughters to see firsthand that forgiveness is possible and crucial. As Christians, we recognize that we do not live in an empty universe, that despite our mistakes or those of others, life is redeemable. Things cannot be undone, but they can be made right. We leave this confidently in God's hands. So, for me forgiveness is really giving myself a beautifully wrapped gift from God...that keeps on giving, and giving, and giving. So, today, I truly wish you well.

Chapter 15 

Release

Years ago, I remember my dad purchasing a live butterfly kit for my daughter that allows you to observe the life cycle of real painted lady butterflies. It had a pop-up butterfly observation habitat and dropper to feed them. There was also a portable caterpillar habitat with larva inside. It was very interesting watching the larvae grow and becoming ten times its original size. We noticed the caterpillars would shed their skin several times before forming a chrysalis, which is the most delicate stage. We observed that the chrysalis turns a very dark color just before the butterfly emerges. After undergoing an amazing transformation, the butterfly begins to pump its wings until stretched out to full size.

PresLee and her Gran Gran were extremely excited to finally open the butterfly habitat and release the butterflies into the sky in our backyard. This process was incredible and would never be forgotten.

I once heard a story about a man who spent hours watching a butterfly struggling to emerge from its cocoon. The butterfly managed to make a small hole, but its body was too large to get through it. After a long struggle, it appeared to be exhausted and remained still. The man decided to help the butterfly, and, with a pair of scissors, he cut open the cocoon, thus releasing the butterfly. However, the butterfly's body was very small and wrinkled, its wings were all crumpled. He continued to watch hoping that the butterfly would open its wings and fly away.

Nothing happened; in fact, the butterfly spent the rest of its brief life dragging around its shrunken body and shriveled wings, incapable of flight. What the man, out of kindness and eagerness to help, had failed to realize, was that the tight cocoon and the efforts that the butterfly had to make in order to squeeze out of that tiny hole were Nature's way of training the butterfly and of strengthening its wings.

Sometimes, a little extra effort is precisely what prepares us for the next phase of our life. Anyone who refuses to make that effort or feels the need to manipulate the situation may prolong the process of transformation. Taking matters into our own hands and not allowing God to control the circumstances can leave us unprepared to fight our next battle and possibly one day even unable to fly.

I didn't want to overstep my boundaries with God and try to fix things that were beyond me. And I found myself overwhelmed by the whole transformation process anyway. The operation that the Great Physician was administering in my life seemed ultimately long and the weight/wait of hope seemed too hard to bear.

I spent numerous hours talking to God, fasting, and praying for others, but still found myself begging God to heal me completely. But everything about me was being taken apart, all the way down to the foundations. I had no control over any of it but was conscious about what was happening to me. I honestly had no choice but to lean into it and wait for the end of the challenging and painful process to come to manifestation. God wasn't finished with me yet; I was restless and needed Him to speak more and more to me each day. This massive change in my soul, would turn out to be one of the most valuable experiences of my life.

Chapter 16 

Courage

The process of a butterfly emerging from its chrysalis is called eclosion. Eclosion is controlled by hormones. These hormones are released to soften the chrysalis and to trigger the central nervous system to begin the movements needed to complete the emergence process. This phase is extremely uncomfortable because it is a restless stage, wanting to break free but not quite ready yet.

Gods timing is perfect and extremely important. Anything other than Gods time, is the wrong time. His timing grows our faith as we are forced to wait and trust in Him and it makes certain that He, and He alone, gets the glory and praise for pulling us through. During this time I am reminded of how human, how natural that when our lives are in ruin we fall on our knees and say "God where are you?", but whenever we're walking in abundance, whenever we have good times, whenever we enjoy the best of success, sometimes we suddenly think, "God I don't need you!" This is a stage that I once found myself in and never intend to go back to. It's not that I intentionally wanted to take God for granted, it's just that I was living a lukewarm Christian life, as it were. You may know what I am talking about. Revelations 3:16 says, "I would wish that you were either hot or you were cold, but because you're not and you're in my body, I want to spew you out of my mouth." Honestly, I prefer The Message Bible's interpretation, "I know you inside and out, and find little to my liking. You're not cold, you're not hot - far better to be either cold or hot! You're stale. You're stagnant. You make me want to vomit." Yes, I was once stale, stagnant, and lukewarm, I wanted to spew my own self out of my mouth for heaven sakes!

I was once a hopeless creature with no goals, no dreams, simply just withering away, floating in stagnant waters, knowing this is not the way life is supposed to be, but doing nothing about it! Nothing, nothing, nothing, the story of my life! Honestly, in my eyes there was nothing God could possibly like about me. But things were about to change, God was about to stir things up a bit. A bit God? In all my nothingness, out of nowhere I come face to face with Satan himself. Surely this is only a dream and soon I will awake. But no, I found myself in the middle of a nightmare pretty much like the one on Elm Street. It was as if I was in a scary movie and Freddy Krueger was at my doorway. Like his victim, Nancy Thompson, Freddy Krueger tried ripping me to shreds with his gloved razor hands, but his cuts of lies, betrayal, and abandonment did not kill me. I woke up! Praise God! I am alive! I survived!!! Job 13:15 says, "Though He slay me, yet will I hope in

Him."

And I am not saying that God sent this insanity my way, what I am saying is that He used this mayhem, this pandemonium to wake me up and help me live again to the fullest! Our world may be facing a crisis with the widespread COVID-19 virus, but it may be no match for the pandemic you find yourself in right now. And no matter what plague is sweeping over you that may seem inescapable or how deep your wounds are, YOU ARE A VICTOR, not a victim!

To all who find themselves at the entrance of that dark and scary road deteriorating inside, who are hesitating to surrender to the darkness that will embrace them, strip them bare and tear them apart until all that is left is the very essence from which to start over, I pray that you will have courage and faith. Those who will stand and trust the Almighty Creator of the Universe with the transformation of their life, will undergo a miraculous transfiguration, that you will never regret.

Chapter 17

Miracle

A caterpillar that metamorphoses into a butterfly creates a chrysalis. A chrysalis usually has a tapered shape and may blend in with the butterfly's habitat and protects the caterpillar as it transforms into adult form. Chrysalis color varies depending on the butterfly species. Interestingly, the chrysalis darkens just before the butterfly emerges. I guess you can say, it gets worse right before the breakthrough.

God had been rebuilding my life and I knew deep inside my being it was almost time to take flight. But just when I thought things were getting brighter, the darkness seeped in, surrounding me, kinda like "uh, uh, no, I'm not finished with you yet!" You see, I received a call from my sister-in-law but only heard a siren in the background. I'll never forget the six words she said, "Get up here quick, it's bad!" All I knew was that I needed to get to my youngest brother not even knowing if he were dead or alive. The only thing I knew to cry out was, "Not today, Satan, not today!" I tried to remain calm on my drive to the hospital. At first, I didn't know how to pray, but the Holy Spirit took over. Then I began to just speak life!

Thank you for touching David's life, Lord!

Thank you, Lord, that David is alive!

I praise You Father that he is alive and well!

Thank you for Your miracles!

Thank you for Your healing!

We praise Your Holy Name, Lord!

You are the Way Maker!

The Miracle Worker!

Thank You Jesus!

I knew what it said in Proverbs 18:21, "that words could kill, or words could give life", and I was expecting life! Also, in Romans 4:17-18 God also said, "Abraham was first named "father" and then became a father because he dared to trust God to do what only God could do: raise the dead to life, with a word make something out of nothing. When everything was hopeless, Abraham believed anyway, deciding to live not on the basis of what he saw he couldn't do but on what God said he would do."

And I remembered the story In John 11, when Jesus finds out that one of His best friends has died. In verses 17-22, "When Jesus finally got there, He found Lazarus already four days dead. Bethany was near Jerusalem, only a couple of miles away, and many of the Jews were visiting Martha and Mary, sympathizing with them over their brother. Martha heard Jesus was coming and went out to meet Him. Mary remained in the house. Martha said, "Master if you'd been here, my brother wouldn't have died. But even now, I know that whatever You ask God He will give you." Wow! So amazing! What faith Martha had in Jesus to have the audacity to say, "but even now" after four whole days! I call this "audacious faith". Jesus called Lazarus to come forth, and he did.

Friends and rescue workers on the scene did everything in their power to save my bother that day when he collapsed and had no pulse or heartbeat. And I remember whispering, "God, if I can only have one miracle, please let it be my brothers healing." It was a rather selfish prayer because I had lost so many things prior that were of importance to me and could not imagine life without him. I will always be grateful for the prayers, verses, and support my brother offered me and my daughters during the most difficult time of our lives but, it was my turn to

David and Dawn.

return the favor and be his prayer warrior and biggest supporter. Although I still needed him, I realized that his family needed him more. And just like Lazarus, Jesus called David to come forth, and he did!

Chapter 18

Stable

Though extremely dark in the chrysalis, I found a sense of comfort. You see, it was familiar, and I knew each pain and suffering by name and date. In this state, I had time to look back and think about my own imperfections born out of making wrong decisions, bad choices, and even circumstances out of my control. Guilt and regret began to weigh heavily on my mind as God revealed my innermost failures and weaknesses that ultimately contributed to my marital wrecking ball experience. My family was completely broken, and my children watched as the marriage was dramatically just thrown away directly in front of them. As heartbreaking and painful as it is to admit, I failed not only as a wife, but as a mother as well, and now my children would pay the price. So, now I am confined in the chrysalis of life I had constructed for myself.

You may find yourself in a similar state. How do we respond when life does not turn out as planned? Do we remain stuck in our cocoons? Many times, the end result is frustration, anger, and isolation. We had grand plans in our lives to accomplish the extraordinary, but then life took a different turn. There is nothing wrong with retreating into a cocoon, as it were, for a little while. Without the cocoon, God's transformation cannot take place. Problems only arise when we make the cocoon our permanent residence. God does not want us to remain stuck. In fact, if a butterfly stays too long in the chrysalis it will die. We go into the cocoon in one state, and then hopefully allow Him to transform our lives by giving us new dreams, goals, and desires. It's not Gods intention to harm us through the process, but to recreate our lives and get us to the point where we can begin to break out of our cocoon to become something even more beautiful and amazing.

Luke 8:11 says that the bible is called a seed, and the seed must be planted in broken ground before it can produce a harvest. If your family, your marriage, your finances, your life, is broken that is exactly where God wants His seed to go so that the harvest of your future is greater than any pain of your past. So, take courage if everything around you has crumbled because God can't use perfect families, perfect marriages, perfect finances, perfect lives, but He can use the many things that are broken.

The struggle was real, and I was struggling to get out of the chrysalis which had engulfed me far too long.

Listening to motivational speakers was a part of my daily routine. One in particular, mentioned that choosing 'one single word' to focus on for a year can help catapult you to a new level. They emphasized the importance of listening to God for that 'one word' and then applying it to every area of your life no matter what time of year. An example, would be the word 'Invest', meaning – to use, to give, to promote time and talent, achieve something. Invest in relationships, family, personal education and growth. Another word might be, 'Purge' – to rid of unwanted feelings or conditions, to release, to be free from anything holding you back, past, old memories etc. Well, I wanted a "word"! And when I asked God about it, immediately the word 'stable' popped into my mind. I thought, what? That sounds stagnant or motionless, so I looked the definition up and loved what it said. 'Stable" – I will not give way, I will not fall; I am firmly fixed, specially designed, sane and sensible; not easily upset or disturbed, well balanced, sound mind, and steady!

This is how I interpret it, "I will not give way to what I see in the natural, I will not fall under financial pressure, I am firmly fixed with my eyes focused on Jesus, I am specially designed by God and have a purpose, I am sane and sensible feasting on Gods Words and wisdom, I am not easily upset or disturbed by the trials that my daughters and I face, I am well balanced and do not let my emotions get the best of me, I have a sound mind and meditate on God's Word, and I am Steady Freddy – no more nightmares for me! Yes, a great 'word' from God! But remember, it took a great 'work' from God to get me to this point in my life. It did not happen overnight, but I am so very grateful for the place He has brought me to. And in the stillness, He is molding me, shaping me, growing me, and stretching me into something wonderful.

When the butterfly emerges, it can no longer carry the extra baggage from its previous state with it. The butterfly must leave behind the days of being a caterpillar and struggling to survive. It must leave all the pains and suffering of its caterpillar days in the ruins of the chrysalis. Only then will it truly be free to fly.

Where are you in your life today? Has life dealt you a bad hand of negative circumstances that are beyond your control, or kicked sand in your face and left you for dead? Maybe your spouse is going through a midlife crisis and decides to leave you behind, or your failures have you feeling unworthy of life. Your prodigal child may have run away and is nowhere to be found, or perhaps you just buried your mom or your dad. Maybe you just received words you did not want to hear, that the diagnosis is cancer and there is no treatment. Are you stuck in a cocoon with seemingly no way out? Well, just like the butterfly we must leave behind the days of being a caterpillar. Shedding resentment, unforgiveness, betrayal, defeat, sadness and hopelessness in the ruins of the chrysalis. Meaning, we must leave all the pain and suffering in God's hands.

When we feel like we are falling, there is but One that can catch us. When we are certain we are drowning, there is but One who lifts us. When we have lost all hope, there is but One who renews and restores us. That One is precious Jesus, the lifter of my head and the lifter of your head too. Psalm 94:16-19 (MSG) says, "The minute I said, "I'm slipping, I'm falling," your love, God, took hold and held me fast. When I was upset and beside myself, you calmed me down and cheered me up." And this same God who takes care of you and me will supply all your needs and all my needs from his glorious riches, which have been given to us in Christ Jesus. Philippians 4:19

As you go through life, keep in mind that 'struggle' is an important part of any growth experience. In fact, it is the 'struggle' that causes you to develop your ability to fly. Now get ready, because at the end of the path there will be sunlight... and wings.

Chapter 19

Metamorphosis

If you look closely at a chrysalis you can see where the eyes and legs are beneath the hard surface. After the chrysalis has been softened and often becomes transparent the butterfly will push through first with its legs also removing the triangular piece covering its eyes and proboscis. The butterfly then crawls the rest of the way out of the chrysalis, exposing the abdomen and wings. The butterfly hangs upside down from the chrysalis or a nearby surface to complete the emergence process. The wings appear folded or crinkled and the butterfly must begin the process of expanding and drying its wings before flight is possible. Meconium is pumped into the venation structures of the wings by wing movement and the help of gravity. Once the wings have fully expanded, the meconium will be pumped back into the body of the butterfly. The small amounts still in the veins of the wings will dry and harden giving the wings a sturdier structure that will allow flight. After the wings have dried out but before the butterfly will take its first flight it will dispel the excess meconium from its body. It was extremely uncomfortable inside the chrysalis, and the urge for me to emerge was massive!

In all of my, what seemed like hopelessness, I began to realize sincerely deep down in my soul that God was truly restoring my shattered life. Reminds me when Ezekiel is given a vision at a time when the nation of Israel is in a hopeless state. The people are in a place where they are lost it seems. In Ezekiel 37:1-14 (MSG) Ezekiel says, "God grabbed me. God's Spirit took me up and set me down in the middle of an open plain strewn with bones. He led me around and among them – a lot of bones! There were bones all over the plain – dry bones, bleached by the sun. He said to me, "Son of man, can these bones live?" I said, "Master God, only you know that." He said to me, "Prophesy over these bones: "Dry bones, listen to the Message of God!" God, the Master, told the dry bones, "Watch this: I'm bringing the breath of life to you and you'll come to life. I'll attach sinew to you and put meat on your bones, cover you with skin, and breathe life into you. You'll come alive and you'll realize that I am God!" I prophesied just as I'd been commanded. As I prophesied, there was a sound and, oh, rustling! The bones moved and came together, bone to bone. I kept watching. Sinews formed, then muscles on the bones, then skin stretched over them. But they had no breath in them. He said to me, "Prophesy to the breath. Prophesy son of man. Tell the breath, 'God, the Master, says, Come from the four winds. Come, breath. Breathe on these slain bodies. Breathe life!" So, I prophesied, just as He commanded me. The breath entered them, and they came alive! They stood up on their feet, a huge army. Then God said to me, "Son of man, these bones are the whole house of Israel. Listen to what they're saying: 'Our bones are dried up, our hope is gone, there's nothing left of us.' Therefore, prophesy. Tell them, God, the Master, says: I'll dig up your graves and bring you out alive – O my people! Then I'll take you straight to the land of Israel. When I dig up graves and bring you out as my people, you'll realize that I am God. I'll breathe my life into you, and you'll live. Then I'll lead you straight back to your land and you'll realize that I am God. I've said it and I'll do it. God's Decree."

Like Israel, it is easy to lose hope when you receive the not so good doctors report, or the job opportunity doesn't work out like you thought it would, or when relationships begin to fall apart. I believe that this text in Ezekiel points out that even in the most hopeless situations, God is still at work and He is able to restore lost hope and rebuild that which is broken, that which lies in ruin. I once read a miraculous story in Readers Digest. It was about a family in which the daughter contracted a form of leukemia that would ultimately kill her unless she received a bone marrow transplant. She had an unusual blood type, which made it extremely difficult to find a donor. Her parents did something unbelievably spectacular.

They began praying to have another child with the same rare blood type. They hoped this second child, would be able to provide the bone marrow needed for their daughter with leukemia. Things were somewhat complicated by the fact that this was an older couple and the man had already had a vasectomy. Not only would doctors need to reverse that, which is a very questionable procedure in itself, but their new baby would need to have the same rare blood type as the older sister. Praise God, it worked! The father's surgery was successful, and the couple were able to conceive again. They gave birth to a second daughter who had the appropriate blood type. After 14 months, the little girl provided enough bone marrow, from her hip, to give a transplant that saved her older sister's life.

So, there is definitely life in the bones. It is important that we do not limit what God can do and what God will do. We must learn to speak life because there is power in the tongue. No matter what your circumstance is just remember that God is still on the throne. God gives hope to the hopeless, purpose to the purposeless and He is still capable, willing, and able to bring life back to old dry bones. So when you call upon Him and say God, restore my family, my business, my marriage, my health, my hopes and dreams, my peace, my joy, it is not a matter of 'if' God restores, it's a matter of 'when' God restores! Hope has a name and its Jesus Christ. In the middle of the valley of hopelessness when it feels like all hope is gone, remember God never leaves your side. God took Ezekiel all around the valley of no hope in dead bones just to let him see the vivid picture. Somehow, we need to see the hopelessness of our situation before we can really see that God will walk us through it. Dare to declare hope! When you feel hopeless, declare it anyway and sing this song...

Dem bones, dem bones gonna walk around.

Dem bones, dem bones gonna walk around.

Dem bones, dem bones gonna walk around.

Oh, hear the Word of the Lord!

God said, "Daun, can this marriage live again?" I said, "Only you know Sovereign Lord, I give it over to you." Remember, it's not over till God says its over!

Chapter 20 

Celebration

Jesus loved to use stories to illustrate profound, life-transforming concepts. In Luke 15 Jesus talks about the prodigal son. He said, "There once was a man who had two sons. The younger son said to his father, 'Father, I want right now what's coming to me.' "So, the father divided the property between them. It wasn't long before the younger son packed his bags and left for a distant country.

There, undisciplined and dissipated, he wasted everything he had. After he had gone through all his money, there was a bad famine all through that country and he began to hurt. He signed on with a citizen there who assigned him to his fields to slop the pigs. He was so hungry he would have eaten the corncobs in the pig slop, but not one would give him any. That brought him to his senses. He said, 'All those farmhands working for my father sit down to three meals a day, and here I am starving to death. I'm going back to my father. I'll say to him, Father, I've sinned against God, I've sinned before you; I don't deserve to be called your son. Take me on as a hired hand.' He got right up and went home to his father.

"When he was still a long way off, his father saw him. His heart pounding, he ran out, embraced him, and kissed him. The son started his speech: 'Father, I've sinned against God, I've sinned before you: I don't deserve to be called your son ever again.' But the father wasn't listening. He was calling to the servants, 'Quick, bring a clean set of clothes and dress him. Put the family ring on his finger and sandals on his feet. Then get a grain-fed heifer and roast it. We're going to feast! We're going to have a wonderful time! My son is here given up for dead and now alive! Given up for lost and now found!' And they began to have a wonderful time."

The life-changing core of the gospel is that when we feel far from God, He is never far from us. I mention this story because just like the prodigal's father, God, my Father and your Father, intends to move Heaven and earth on our behalf, too. No matter what you've done or where you've been, God is the ultimate Dad of second chances. The moment we turn back toward Him, He runs out to meet us. No matter how long your prodigal child or spouse has been gone, or what turmoil your finances are in, no matter how broken your family is, how impossible your job situation seems, or how incurable your disease is, God is for you, not against you. I love The Message Bibles translation of Romans 8:31-39, it says, "So, what do you think? With God on our side like this, how can we lose? If God didn't hesitate to put everything on the line for us, embracing our condition and exposing himself to the worst by sending his own Son, is there anything else he wouldn't gladly and freely do for us?

And who would dare tangle with God by messing with one of God's chosen? Who would dare even to point a finger? The One who died for us-who was raised to life for us! – is in the presence of God at this very moment sticking up for us. Do you think anyone is going to be able to drive a wedge between us and Christ's love for us? There is no way! Not trouble, not hard times, not hatred, not hunger, not homelessness, not bullying threats, not backstabbing, not even the worst sins listed in Scripture: They kill us in cold blood because they hate you. We're sitting ducks; they pick us off one by one. None of this fazes us because Jesus loves us. I'm absolutely convinced that nothing-nothing living or dead, angelic or demonic, today or tomorrow, high or low, thinkable or unthinkable-absolutely nothing can get between us and God's love because of the way that Jesus our Master has embraced us."

(Mic drop!)

The truth of the matter is that it rains on the just and the unjust. But the good news is, when it is raining on the just, "Our God is a refuge and strength and ever present help in a time of trouble." Psalm 46:1-3 The Message Bible translates it like this, "God is a safe place to hide, ready to help when we need him. We stand fearless at the cliff-edge of doom, courageous in sea storm and earthquake, before the rush and roar of oceans, the tremors that shift mountains. Jacob-wrestling God fights for us, God-of-Angel-Armies protects us."

As uncertain as things are God almighty is still on His throne. He is a healer, faithful, and all sufficient, His angels have charge over you and me, He protects us. And as a child of God we have this promise to hold on to in every situation that we face in life, Romans 8:28, "And we know that all things work together for good to them that love God, to them who are the called according to his purpose." Your outlook on life determines your outcome in life. So today Lord, I release what I think my heart wants....and accept Your outcome! Thank you Lord, I am free! I can breathe, I can breathe, I can breathe!

Chapter 21 

Restoration

While writing this book I prayed diligently that God would give me the words to say before beginning every chapter. He has never failed to inspire my heart and lead me in the direction I should go. But chapter 21, the final chapter, was a little different. It was unfamiliar territory because I still felt a little stuck inside the chrysalis to some extent. Honestly, I wanted OUT, I was raring to fly! There was such an overwhelming, antsy feeling in my body to completely break free from this long winter's nap I found myself taking. I began walking and running daily and found myself chanting this little cheer/song that I made up and intentionally reminding God that I was ready to soar!

I'm walking, and walking.

In abundance, in abundance.

Walking by faith, not by sight,

walking by faith, not by sight.

Faith over fear, faith over fear!

This is the day that the Lord has made,

I will rejoice and be glad in it.

I will enter His gates with thanksgiving in my heart,

I will enter His courts with praise.

Rejoice in the Lord, rejoice in the Lord,

For He hath made me glad!

Repeat- but this time I'm running, I'm running.

I love how The Passion Bible translates James 1:2-4. It says, "My fellow believers, when it seems as though you are facing nothing, but difficulties seek it as an invaluable opportunity to experience the greatest 'joy' that you can!" What?? Yes! "For you know that when your faith is tested it stirs up power within you to endure all things. And then as your endurance grows even stronger it will release perfection into every part of your being until there is nothing missing and nothing lacking." And boy, did I feel the power of God in my life, and I was ready to be released into the perfection of His beautifully painted sky. He most certainly had been doing a great work within the chrysalis of my being.

Daily, I repeated this..." Thank you Lord that today I have joy unspeakable and full of glory, thank you Lord that today I have joy unspeakable and full of glory, thank you Lord that today I have joy unspeakable and full of glory!"

Another cheer/chant I repeat daily as I *walk and talk with God goes something like this…*

This is my battle cry, this is my battle cry.

Thy will be done; X Thy will be done. XX

Not my way…no way, X not my way…no way! XX

Your will and Your way, oh yeah, Your will and Your way.

Uh huh!

I trust God, I trust God

with an exclamation point, X exclamation point! XX

I release what I think I want

and accept Your outcome X and accept Your outcome. XX

Thy will be done, X Thy will be done! XX

And repeat…

I was not sure how to complete the last chapter in my book because I wasn't sure if God had completed me. You see my marriage wasn't restored yet and it was important that my daughters see a miraculous miracle of all the broken pieces put back together. Interestingly, one night I had a dream about the man at the pool of Bethesda.

John 5:1-8 says, "Then Jesus returned to Jerusalem to

observe one of the Jewish holy days. Inside the city near the Sheep Gate there is a pool called in Aramaic, The House of Loving Kindness. And this pool is surrounded by five covered porches. Hundreds of sick people were lying there on the porches- the paralyzed, the blind, and the crippled, all of them waiting for their healing. For an angel of God would periodically descend into the pool to stir the waters, and the first one who stepped into the pool after the waters swirled would instantly be healed.

Now there was a man who had been disabled for thirty-eight years lying among the multitude of the sick. When Jesus saw him lying there, He knew that the man had been crippled for a long time. So, Jesus said to him, "Do you truly long to be healed?" The sick man answered him, "Sir, there's no way I can get healed, for I have no one who will lower me into the water when the angel comes. As soon as I try to crawl to the edge of the pool, someone else jumps in ahead of me." Then Jesus said to him, "Stand up! Pick up your sleeping mat and walk!" And that's exactly what he did.

Funny work story... The Executive Director of the company I work for is such a kind and warm-hearted individual who is very complimentary. In fact, he sometimes compliments me on particular outfits that I wear. Since I am not very good at receiving compliments, I usually try to respond in a funny way. So, if he were to say, "That is a pretty dress you are wearing today.", I might say something like, "Oh, this is my Amish dress or this is my Little House on the Prairie dress." Once I even pointed to my outfit and said, "Cat Woman" and, "80's prom." haha I'm just being silly, I know.

Recently, my Supervisor and close friend, Vickie placed a fall looking plant at the front desk where I sit. Those passing by noticed the Autumn foliage, which was designed and assembled in quite a unique way, and offered their opinions concerning it. Some found the arrangement quite interesting but many bluntly stated that they did not like it.

Also, not long ago, a sweet co- worker named Courtney walked by the front desk and told me she liked my dress, that I reminded her of Tinkerbell. Lol Then, while pointing to this widely discussed plant said, "You remind me of this." My eyes almost popped out of my head because I was aware of the front desk 'plant controversy'.

Front Desk Arrangement

But much to my amazement she was touching the Peacock feather which was lodged down right smack in the middle of the floral arrangement. Now, I said all that... to say this...When I think of a peacock feather, I think of strength, beauty and the confidence that the peacock exhibits. 2 Corinthians 5:17 (TPT) says, "Now, if anyone is enfolded into Christ, he has become an entirely new creation. All that is related to the old order has vanished. Behold, everything is fresh and new." I honestly believe that the peacock feather symbolizes a true miracle, the restoration of 'my life'. And oh boy, did my daughters get to witness it firsthand. A completely broken vessel scattered into a million, tiny pieces, miraculously resurrected by the mighty hand of God! There was no longer a lifeless, frail female hanging on by a thread to the chrysalis of life, believing she was too old, and that her life was over. But now, standing confident and tall like a peacock, my daughters see a strong, faith filled, powerful, Christlike woman with purpose and determination, ready to break free and soar to new heights.

I know, you too have been there and are experiencing similar afflictions while undergoing a transfiguration. One thing I have learned is that affliction builds faith and is truly good for our soul. Psalm 119:71 (TPT) David says, "The affliction you brought me through was the best thing that could have happened to me, for it taught me your ways." I would like to leave with you a few encouraging words that I hold dear to my heart.

If I had never needed anything, I wouldn't have known that God was my provider.

If I had never felt my life was over then I would never have learned how to pray, really pray.

If I had never been abandoned, then I would have never learned to depend upon my Lord.

If I had never been hungry or thirsty then I would have never known that God is my Bread of Life and Living Water.

If I had never been sick and broken, I would never have known that God is the Great Physician.

If I had never been sick and broken, I would never have known that God is the Great Physician.

If I had never been betrayed, then I would have never run so fast into the arms of Jesus.

He is truly Jehovah Jireh, my Provider.

Lastly my prayer for you comes from (TPT), Philippians 1:6 , *"I pray with great faith for you, because I'm fully convinced that the One who began this glorious work in you will faithfully continue the process of maturing you and will put his finishing touches to it until the unveiling of our Lord Jesus Christ!"*

And just like the man at the pool of Bethesda, Jesus saw me lying there, and He knew I had been there for a while. So, Jesus asked me, "Daun, do you truly long to be free?" I said, "Sir, I have crawled out to the edge but I'm not sure what's next." Then I heard Jesus whisper, "Take a deep breath, be not afraid and RISE UP! It's time to spread your wings... and FLY."

So that's exactly what I did...

The Beginning

A Message from the Author

Dear Friend,

Thank you for sharing this journey of hope and healing with me. I am truly humbled and honored to have had you travel along side of me during, not only one of the most difficult times of my life, but during the beautiful restoration of my life.

If God can do this for me, He can surely transform your life as well.

My prayer for you is found in

Numbers 6:24-26 (NLT)

"May the Lord bless you

and protect you.

May the Lord smile on you

and be gracious to you.

May the Lord show you His favor

and give you His peace."

Always,

Daun

About the Author

Daun was born in Whiteman AFB, Missouri and is considered a 'military brat' due to her dad serving full time in the United States Air Force. A military brat is not considered to be a pejorative (as in describing a spoiled child), but rather connotes affection and respect. Due to a lifestyle of constantly moving, and immersion in military culture, she frequently felt like an outsider in relation to the civilian culture. As her family traveled from base to base, never having a hometown, she found that she really had no place to call home.

While growing up the author was quite timid and self-conscious. Moving from one school to another, leaving friends behind, seemed to be a normal way of life. Holding deep within what seemed like a myriad of emotions made writing a means of escape.

She began writing poems, songs and children's books at an early age. During her teens, she found that her voice was the instrument of her deepest feelings. She took vocal lessons and began singing in churches and at other functions and events. She enjoyed traveling and performing with several singing groups and Drama Teams throughout the State of Alabama and surrounding areas. She even taught voice lessons for many years.

After getting married and having two beautiful daughters, HeartLee and PresLee, she found herself living a peaceful and content life teaching Kindergarten, Music and Drama at Crenshaw Christian Academy in Luverne, Al for almost 30 years. CCA was the first place that the author was really able to finally call *home*. Daun also enjoyed her short stay at Luverne High School teaching Collaborative Reading to elementary students. Coaching Cheerleading and Dance Teams throughout her teaching career is something she truly loved to do. The memories of all her many students over the years will always remain close inside her heart.

In 2008, she was honored and recognized as the (AISA)- Alabama Independent School Association, Teacher of the Year. Today she works as a Public Relations Representative in Montgomery Al along with teaching Chinese students to speak English online.

Just

when the

caterpillar

thought her life

was over...

She began to fly.

"But thanks be to God, who gives us the victory through our Lord Jesus Christ."

1 Corinthians 15:57

Made in the USA
Columbia, SC
11 March 2021

34163609R00075